Peter Handke

# OFFENDING THE AUDIENCE
## and
# SELF-ACCUSATION

*translated by Michael Roloff*

GW00673697

METHUEN & CO LTD
11 NEW FETTER LANE · LONDON EC4

# Contents

In translating the invective at the end of *Offending the Audience*, I translated the principle according to which they are arranged – that is, I sought to create new acoustic patterns in English – rather than translate each epithet literally, which would only have resulted in completely discordant patterns. In nearly every other respect these are translations and not adaptations. Peter Handke himself has cut the last sentence in *Self-Accusation*.

M.R.

NOTE ON *Offending the Audience*
AND *Self-Accusation*

The speak-ins (*Sprechstücke*) are spectacles without pictures, inasmuch as they give no picture of the world. They point to the world not by way of pictures but by way of words; the words of the speak-ins don't point at the world as something lying outside the words but to the world in the words themselves. The words that make up the speak-ins give no picture of the world but a concept of it. The speak-ins are theatrical inasmuch as they employ natural forms of expression found in reality. They employ only such expressions as are natural in real speech; that is, they employ the speech forms that are uttered *orally* in real life. The speak-ins employ natural examples of swearing, of self-indictment, of confession, of testimony, of interrogation, of justification, of evasion, of prophecy, of calls for help. Therefore they need a vis-à-vis, at least *one* person who listens; otherwise, they would not be natural but extorted by the author. It is to that extent that my speak-ins are pieces for the theatre. Ironically, they imitate the gestures of all the given devices natural to the theatre.

The speak-ins have no action, since every action on stage would only be the picture of another action. The speak-ins confine themselves, by obeying their natural form, to words. They give no pictures, not even pictures in word form, which would only be pictures the author extorted to represent an internal, unexpressed, wordless circumstance and not a *natural* expression.

Speak-ins are autonomous prologues to the old plays. They do not want to revolutionize, but to make aware.

*Peter Handke*

Offending the Audience *was first produced in Britain at the Oval House, London, in December 1970 by The Other Company. The cast were: Jane Bond, Judy Monahan, Andrew Norton and Robert Walker; directed by Naftali Yavin.*

# Offending the Audience

*for Karlheinz Braun, Claus Peymann, Basch Peymann, Wolfgang Wiens, Peter Steinbach, Michael Gruner, Ulrich Hass, Claus Dieter Reents, Rüdiger Vogler, John Lennon*

*Rules for the actors*

Listen to the litanies in the Catholic churches.

Listen to football teams being cheered on and booed.

Listen to the rhythmic chanting at demonstrations.

Listen to the wheels of a bicycle upturned on its seat spinning until the spokes have come to rest and watch the spokes until they have reached their resting point.

Listen to the gradually increasing noise a concrete mixer makes after the motor has been started.

Listen to debaters cutting each other off.

Listen to 'Tell Me' by the Rolling Stones.

Listen to the simultaneous arrival and departure of trains.

Listen to the hit parade on Radio Luxembourg.

Listen in on the simultaneous interpreters at the United Nations.

Listen to the dialogue between the gangster (Lee J. Cobb) and the pretty girl in 'The Trap', when the girl asks the gangster how many more people he intends to kill; whereupon the gangster asks, as he leans back, How many are left? and watch the gangster as he says it.

See the Beatles' movies.

In 'A Hard Day's Night' watch Ringo's smile at the moment when, after having been teased by the others, he sits down at his drums and begins to play.

Watch Gary Cooper's face in 'The Man From the West'. In the same movie watch the death of the mute as he runs down the deserted street of the lifeless town with a bullet in him, hopping and jumping and emitting those shrill screams.

Watch monkeys aping people and llamas spitting in the zoo.

Watch the behaviour of tramps and idlers as they amble on the street and play the machines in the penny arcades.

*When the theatregoers enter the room into which they are meant to go, they are greeted by the usual pre-performance atmosphere. One might let them hear noises from behind the curtain, noises that make believe that scenery is being shifted about. For example, a table is dragged across the stage, or several chairs are noisily set up and then removed. One might let the spectators in the first few rows hear directions whispered by make-believe stage managers and the whispered interchanges between make-believe stagehands behind the curtain. Or, even better, use tape recordings of other performances in which, before the curtain rises, objects are really shifted about. These noises should be amplified to make them more audible, and perhaps should be stylized and arranged so as to produce their own order and uniformity.*

*The usual theatre atmosphere should prevail. The ushers should be more assiduous than usual, even more formal and ceremonious, should subdue their usual whispering with even more style, so that their behaviour becomes infectious. The programmes should be elegant. The bell signals should not be forgotten; the signals are repeated at successively briefer intervals. The gradual dimming of the lights should be even more gradual if possible; perhaps the lights can be dimmed in successive stages. As the ushers proceed to close the doors, their gestures should become particularly solemn and noticeable. Yet, they are only ushers. Their actions should not appear symbolic. Latecomers should not be admitted. Inappropriately dressed ticket holders should not be admitted. The concept of what is sartorially inappropriate should be strictly applied. None of the spectators should call attention to himself or offend the eye by his attire. The men should be dressed in dark jackets, with white shirts and inconspicuous ties. The women should shun bright colours.*

*There is no standing-room. Once the doors are closed and the lights dim, it gradually becomes quiet behind the curtain too. The silence behind the curtain and the silence in the auditorium are alike. The spectators stare a while longer at the almost imperceptibly fluttering curtain, which may perhaps billow once or twice as though someone had hurriedly crossed the stage. Then the curtain grows still. There is a short pause. The curtain slowly rises, allowing an unobstructed view. Once the stage is completely open to view, the four speakers step forward from upstage. Nothing impedes their progress. The stage is empty. As they walk forward non-committally, dressed casually, it becomes light on stage as well as in the audience. The light on stage and in the auditorium is of the same intensity as at the end of a performance and there is no glare to hurt the eyes. The stage and the auditorium remain lighted throughout the performance. Even as they approach, the speakers don't look at the audience. They don't direct the words they are speaking at the audience. Under no circumstance should the audience get the impression that the words are directed at them. As far as the speakers are concerned, the audience does not yet exist. As they approach, they move their lips. Gradually their words became intelligible and finally they become loud. The invectives they deliver overlap one another. The speakers speak pell-mell. They pick up each other's words. They take words out of each other's mouths. They speak in unison, each uttering different words. They repeat. They grow louder. They scream. They pass rehearsed words from mouth to mouth. Finally, they rehearse one word in unison. The words they use in this prologue are the following (their order is immaterial):* You chuckle-heads, you small-timers, you nervous nellies, you fuddy-duddies, you windbags, you sitting ducks, you milksops. *The speakers should strive for a certain acoustic uniformity. However, except for the acoustic pattern, no other picture should be produced. The invectives are not directed at anyone in particular. The manner of their delivery should not induce a meaning. The speakers reach the front of the stage before they finish rehearsing their invectives. They stand at ease but form a sort of pattern. They are not completely fixed in their positions but move according to the movement which the words they speak lend them. They now look at the public, but at no one person in particular. They are silent for a while. They collect themselves. Then they begin to speak. The order in which they speak is immaterial. The speakers have roughly the same amount of work to do.*

You are welcome.

This piece is a prologue.

You will hear nothing you have not heard here before.
You will see nothing you have not seen here before.
You will see nothing of what you have always seen here.
You will hear nothing of what you have always heard here.

You will hear what you usually see.
You will hear what you usually don't see.
You will see no spectacle.
Your curiosity will not be satisfied.
You will see no play.
There will be no playing here tonight.
You will see a spectacle without pictures.

You expected something.
You expected something else perhaps.
You expected objects.
You expected no objects.
You expected an atmosphere.
You expected a different world.
You expected no different world.
In any case, you expected something.
It may be the case that you expected what you are hearing now.
But even in that case you expected something different.

You are sitting in rows. You form a pattern. You are sitting in a certain order. You are facing in a certain direction. You are sitting equidistant from one another. You are an audience. You form a unit. You are auditors and spectators in an auditorium. Your thoughts are free. You can still make up your own mind. You see us speaking and you hear us speaking. You are beginning to breathe in one and the same rhythm. You are beginning to breathe in one and the same rhythm in which we are speaking. You are breathing the way we are speaking. We and you gradually form a unit.

You are not thinking. You don't think of anything. You are thinking along. You are not thinking along. You feel uninhibited. Your thoughts are free. Even as we say that, we insinuate ourselves into your thoughts. You have thoughts in the back of your mind. Even as we say that, we insinuate ourselves into the thoughts in the back of your mind. You are thinking along. You are hearing. Your thoughts are following in the track of our thoughts. Your thoughts are not following in the track of our thoughts. You are not thinking. Your thoughts are not free. You feel inhibited.

You are looking at us when we speak to you. You are not watching us. You are looking at us. You are being looked at. You are unprotected. You no longer have the advantage of looking from the shelter of darkness into the light. We no longer have the disadvantage of looking through the blinding light into the dark. You are not watching. You are looking at and you are being looked at. In this way, we and you gradually form a unit. Under certain conditions, therefore, we, instead of saying *you*, could say *we*. We are under one and the same roof. We are a closed society.

You are not listening to us. You heed us. You are no longer eavesdropping from behind a wall. We are speaking directly to you. Our dialogue no longer moves at right angles to your glance. Your glance no longer pierces our dialogue. Our words and your glances no longer form an angle. You are not disregarded. You are not treated as mere hecklers. You need not form an opinion from a bird's or a frog's perspective of anything that happens here. You need not play referee. You are no longer treated as spectators to whom we can speak in asides. This is no play. There are no asides here. Nothing that takes place here is intended as an appeal to you. This is no play. We don't step out of the play to address you. We have no need of illusions to disillusion you. We show you nothing. We are playing no destinies. We are playing no dreams. This is not a factual report. This is no documentary play. This is no slice of life. We don't tell you a story. We don't perform any actions. We don't simulate any actions. We don't represent anything. We don't put anything on for you. We only speak. We play by addressing you. When we say we, we may also mean you. We are not acting out your situation. You cannot recognize yourselves in us. We are playing no situation. You need not feel that we mean you. You cannot feel that we mean you. No mirror is being held up to you. We don't mean you. We are addressing you. You are being addressed. You will be addressed. You will be bored if you don't want to be addressed.

You are sharing no experience. You are not sharing. You are not following suit. You are experiencing no intrigues here. You are experiencing nothing. You are not imagining anything. You don't have to imagine anything. You need no prerequisites. You don't need to know that this is a stage. You need no expectations. You need not lean back expectantly. You don't need to know that this is only playing. We make up no stories. You are not following an event. You are not playing along. You are being played with here. That is a wordplay.

What is the theatre's is not rendered unto the theatre here. Here you don't receive your due. Your curiosity is not satisfied. No spark will leap across from us to you. You will not be electrified. These boards don't signify a world. They are part of the world. These boards exist for us to stand on. This world is no different from yours. You are no longer eavesdroppers. You are the subject matter. The focus is on you. You are in the crossfire of our words.

This is no mirage. You don't see walls that tremble. You don't hear the spurious sounds of doors snapping shut. You hear no sofas squeaking. You see no apparitions. You have no visions. You see no picture of something. Nor do you see the suggestion of a picture. You see no picture puzzle. Nor do you see an empty picture. The emptiness of this stage is no picture of another emptiness. The emptiness of this stage signifies nothing. This stage is empty because objects would be in our way. It is empty because we don't need objects. This stage represents nothing. It represents no other emptiness. This stage *is* empty. You don't see any objects that pretend to be other objects. You don't see a darkness that pretends to be another darkness. You don't see a brightness that pretends to be another brightness. You don't see any light that pretends to be another light. You don't hear any noise that pretends to be another noise. You don't see a room that pretends to be another room. Here you are not experiencing a time that pretends to be another time. The time on stage is no different from the time off stage. We have the same local time here. We are in the same location. We are breathing the same air. The front of the stage is not a line of demarcation. It is not only sometimes no demarcation line. It is no demarcation line as long as we are speaking to you. There is no invisible circle here. There is no magic circle. There is no room for play here. We are not playing. We are all in the same room. The demarcation line has not been penetrated, it is not pervious, it doesn't even exist. There is no radiation belt between you and us. We are not self-propelled stage props. We are no pictures of something. We are no representatives. We represent nothing. We demonstrate nothing. We have no pseudonyms. Our heartbeat does not pretend to be another's heartbeat. Our bloodcurdling screams don't pretend to be another's bloodcurdling screams. We don't step out of our roles. We have no roles. We are ourselves. We are the mouthpiece of the author. You cannot make yourself a picture of us. You don't need to make yourself a picture of us. We are ourselves. Our opinion and the author's opinion are not necessarily the same.

The light that illuminates us signifies nothing. Neither do the clothes we wear signify anything. They indicate nothing, they are not unusual in any way, they signify nothing. They signify no other time to you, no other climate, no other season, no other degree of latitude, no other reason to wear them. They have no function. Nor do our gestures have a function, that is, to signify something to you. This is not the world as a stage.

We are no slapstick comedians. There are no objects here that we might trip over. Insidious objects are not on the programme. Insidious objects are not part of the play because we are not playing with them. The objects are not intended to be insidious; they are insidious. If we happen to trip, we trip unwittingly. Unwitting as well are mistakes in dress; unwitting, too, are our perhaps foolish faces. Slips of the tongue, which amuse you, are not intended. If we stutter, we stutter without meaning to. We cannot make dropping a handkerchief part of the play. We are not playing. We cannot make the insidiousness of objects part of the play. We cannot camouflage the insidiousness of objects. We cannot be of two minds. We cannot be of many minds. We are no clowns. We are not in the ring. You don't have the pleasure of encircling us. You are not enjoying the comedy of having a rear view of us. You are not enjoying the comedy of insidious objects. You are enjoying the comedy of words.

The possibilities of the theatre are not exploited here. The realm of possibilities is not exhausted. The theatre is not unbounded. The theatre is bound. Fate is meant ironically here. We are not theatrical. Our comedy is not overwhelming. Your laughter cannot be liberating. We are not playful. We are not playing a world for you. This is not half of one world. We and you do not constitute two halves.

You are the subject matter. You are the centre of interest. No actions are performed here, you are being acted upon. That is no wordplay. You are not treated as individuals here. You don't become individuals here. You have no individual traits. You have no distinctive physiognomies. You are not individuals here. You have no characteristics. You have no destiny. You have no history. You have no past. You are on no wanted list. You have no experience of life. You have the experience of the theatre here. You have that certain something. You are playgoers. You are of no interest because of your capacities. You are of interest solely in your capacity as playgoers. As playgoers you form a pattern here. You are no personalities. You are not singular. You are a plurality of persons. Your faces point in one direction. You are an event. You are *the* event.

You are under review by us. But you form no picture. You are not symbolic. You are an ornament. You are a pattern. You have features that everyone here has. You have general features. You are a species. You form a pattern. You are doing and you are not doing the same thing: you are looking in one direction. You don't stand up and look in different directions. You are a standard pattern and you have a pattern as a standard. You have a standard with which you came to the theatre. You have the standard idea that where we are is up and where you are is down. You have the standard idea of two worlds. You have the standard idea of the world of the theatre.

You don't need this standard now. You are not attending a piece for the theatre. You are not attending. You are the focal point. You are in the crossfire. You are being inflamed. You can catch fire. You don't need a standard. You are the standard. You have been discovered. You are the discovery of the evening. You inflame us. Our words catch fire on you. From you a spark leaps across to us.

This room does not make believe it is a room. The side that is open to you is not the fourth wall of a house. The world does not have to be cut open here. You don't see any doors here. You don't see the two doors of the old dramas. You don't see the back door through which he who shouldn't be seen can slip out. You don't see the front door through which he who wants to see him who shouldn't be seen enters. There is no back door. Neither is there a non-existent door as in modern drama. The non-existent door does not represent a non-existent door. This is not another world. We are not pretending that you don't exist. You are not thin air for us. You are of crucial importance to us because you exist. We are speaking to you because you exist. If you did not exist, we would be speaking to thin air. Your existence is not simply taken for granted. You don't watch us through a keyhole. We don't pretend that we are alone in the world. We don't explain ourselves to our-selves only in order to put you in the know. We are not conducting an exhibition purely for the benefit of your enlightenment. We need no artifice to enlighten you. We need no tricks. We don't have to be theatrically effective. We have no entrances, we have no exits, we don't talk to you in asides. We are putting nothing over on you. We are not about to enter into a dialogue. We are not in a dialogue. Nor are we in a dialogue with you. We have no wish to enter into a dialogue with you. You are not in collusion with us. You are not eyewitnesses to an event. We are not taunting you. You don't have to be apathetic any more. You don't have to watch inactively any more. No actions take place here. You feel the dis-comfort of being watched and addressed, since you came prepared to watch and make yourselves comfortable in the shelter of the dark. Your presence is every moment explicitly acknowledged with every one of our words. Your presence is the topic we deal with from one breath to the next, from one moment to the next, from one word to the next. Your standard idea of the theatre is no longer presupposed as the basis of our actions. You are neither condemned to watch nor free to watch. You are the subject. You are the play-makers. You are the counterplotters. You are being aimed at. You are the target of our words. You serve as targets. That is a metaphor. You serve as the target of our metaphors. You serve as metaphors.

Of the two poles here, you are the pole at rest. You are in an arrested state. You find yourselves in a state of expectation. You are no subjects. You are objects here. You are the objects of our words. Still, you are subjects too.

There are no intervals here. The intervals between words lack significance. Here the unspoken word lacks significance. There are no unspoken words here. Our silences say nothing. There is no deafening silence. There is no silent silence. There is no deathly quiet. Speech is not used to create silence here. This play includes no direction telling us to be silent. We make no artificial pauses. Our pauses are natural pauses. Our pauses are not eloquent like speech. We say nothing with our silence. No abyss opens up between words. You cannot read anything between our lines. You cannot read anything in our faces. Our gestures express nothing of consequence to anything. What is inexpressible is not said through silences here. Glances and gestures are not eloquent here. Becoming silent and being silent is no artifice here. There are no silent letters here. There's only the mute *h*. That is a pun.

You have made up your minds now. You have recognized that we negate something. You have recognized that we repeat ourselves. You have recognized that we contradict ourselves. You have recognized that this piece is conducting an argument with the theatre. You have recognized the dialectical structure of the piece. You have recognized a certain spirit of contrariness. The intention of the piece has become clear to you. You have recognized that we primarily negate. You have recognized that we repeat ourselves. You recognize. You see through. You have not made up your minds. You have not seen through the dialectical structure of the piece. Now you are seeing through. Your thoughts were one thought too slow. Now you have thoughts in the back of your mind.

You look charming. You look enchanting. You look dazzling. You look breathtaking. You look unique.

But you don't make an evening. You're not a brilliant idea. You are tiresome. You are not a rewarding subject. You are a theatrical blunder. You are not true to life. You are not theatrically effective. You don't send us. You don't enchant us. You don't dazzle us. You don't entertain us fabulously. You are not playful. You are not sprightly. You have no tricks up your sleeve. You have no flair for the theatre. You have nothing to say. Your début is unconvincing. You are not with it. You don't help us pass the time. You are not addressing the human quality in us. You leave us cold.

This is no drama. No action that has occurred elsewhere is re-enacted here. Only a now and a now and a now exist here. This is no make-believe which re-enacts an action that really happened once upon a time. Time plays no role here. We are not acting out a plot. Therefore we are not playing time. Time is for real here, it expires from one word to the next. Time flies in the words here. It is not alleged that time can be repeated here. No play can be repeated here and play at the same time it did once upon a time. The time here is *your* time. Space time here is your space time. Here you can compare your time with our time. Time is no noose. That is no make-believe. It is not alleged here that time can be repeated. The umbilical cord connecting you to your time is not severed here. Time is not at play here. We mean business with time here. It is admitted here that time expires from one word to the next. It is admitted that this is *your* time here. You can check the time here on your watches. No other time governs here. The time that governs here is measured against your breath. Time conforms to your wishes here. We measure time by your breath, by the batting of your eyelashes, by your pulsebeats, by the growth of your cells. Time expires here from moment to moment. Time is measured in moments. Time is measured in your moments. Time goes through your stomach. Time here is not repeatable as in the make-believe of a theatre performance. This is no performance: you have not to imagine anything. Time is no noose here. Time is not cut off from the outside world here. There are no two levels of time here. There are no two worlds here. While we are here, the earth continues to turn. Our time up here is your time down there. It expires from one word to the next. It expires while we, we and you, are breathing, while our hair is growing, while we are sweating, while we are smelling, while we are hearing. Time is not repeatable even if we repeat our words, even if we mention again that our time is your time, that it expires from one word to the next, while we, we and you, are breathing, while our hair is growing, while we sweat, while we smell, while we hear. We cannot repeat anything, time is expiring. It is unrepeatable. Each moment is historical. Each of your moments is a historical moment. We cannot say our words twice. This is no make-believe. We cannot do the same thing once again. We cannot repeat the same gestures. We cannot speak the same way. Time expires on our lips. Time is unrepeatable. Time is no noose. That is no make-believe. The past is not made contemporaneous. The past is dead and buried. We need no puppet to embody a dead time. This is no puppet show. This is no nonsense. This is no play. This is no sense. You recognize the contradiction. Time here serves the wordplay.

This is no manœuvre. This is no exercise for the emergency. No one has to play dead here. No one has to pretend he is alive. Nothing is posited here. The number of wounded is not prescribed. The result is not predetermined on paper. There is no

result here. No one has to present himself here. We don't represent
except what we are. We don't represent ourselves in a state
other than the one we are in now and here. This is no manœuvre.
We are not playing ourselves in different situations. We are not
thinking of the emergency. We don't have to represent our death.
We don't have to represent our life. We don't play ahead of time
what and how we will be. We make no future contemporaneous
in our play. We don't represent another time. We don't represent the emergency. We are speaking while time expires. We
speak of the expiration of time. We are not acting as if. We are not
acting as if we could repeat time or as if we could anticipate time.
This is neither make-believe nor a manœuvre. On the other hand
we do act as if. We act as if we could repeat words. We appear
to repeat ourselves. Here is the world of appearances. Here
appearance is appearance. Appearance is here appearance.

You represent something. You are someone. You are something.
You are not someone here but something. You are a society that
represents an order. You are a theatre society of sorts. You are an
order because of your kind of dress, the position of your bodies,
the direction of your glances. The colour of your clothes clashes
with the colour of your seating arrangement. You also form an
order with the seating arrangement. You are dressed up. With
your dress you observe an order. You dress up. By dressing up,
you demonstrate that you are doing something that you don't do
every day. You are putting on a masquerade so as to partake of a
masquerade. You partake. You watch. You stare. By watching,
you become rigid. The seating arrangement favours this develop-
ment. You are something that watches. You need room for your
eyes. If the curtain comes down, you gradually become claustro-
phobic. You have no vantage point. You feel encircled. You feel
inhibited. The rising of the curtain merely relieves your claustro-
phobia. Thus it relieves you. You can watch. Your view is unobstructed. You become uninhibited. You can partake. You are
not in dead centre as when the curtain is closed. You are no longer

someone. You become something. You are no longer alone with yourselves. You are no longer left to your own devices. Now you are with it. You are an audience. That is a relief. You can partake.

Up here there is no order now. There are no objects that demonstrate an order to you. The world here is neither sound nor unsound. This is no world. Stage props are out of place here. Their positions are not chalked out on the stage. Since they are not chalked out, there is no order here. There are no chalk marks for the standpoint of things. There are no memory props for the standpoint of persons. In contrast to you and your seating arrangement, nothing is in its place here. Things here have no fixed places like the places of your seating arrangements down there. This stage is no world, just as the world is no stage.

Nor does each thing have its own time here. No thing has its own time here. No thing has its fixed time here when it serves as a prop or when it becomes an obstacle. We don't act as if things were really used. Here things *are* useful.

You are not standing. You are using the seating arrangements. You are sitting. Since your seating arrangements form a pattern, you form a pattern as well. There is no standing-room. People enjoy art more effectively when they sit than if they stand. That is why you are sitting. You are friendlier when you sit. You are more receptive. You are more open-minded. You are more long-suffering. Sitting, you are more relaxed. You are more democratic. You are less bored. Time seems less long and boring to you. You allow more to happen to you. You are more clairvoyant. You are less distracted. It is easier for you to forget your surroundings. The world around you disappears more easily. You begin to resemble one another more. You begin to lose your personal qualities. You begin to lose the characteristics that distinguish you from each other. You become a unit. You become a pattern. You become one. You lose your self-consciousness. You become spectators.

You become auditors. You become apathetic. You become all eyes and ears. You forget to look at your watch. You forget yourself.

Standing, you would be more effective hecklers. In view of the anatomy of the human body, your heckling would be louder if you stood. You would be better able to clench your fists. You could show your opposition better. You would have greater mobility. You would not need to be as well-behaved. You could shift your weight from one foot to the other. You could more easily become conscious of your body. Your enjoyment of art would be diminished. You would no longer form a pattern. You would no longer be rigid. You would lose your geometry. You would be better able to smell the sweat of the bodies near you. You would be better able to express agreement by nudging each other. If you stood, the sluggishness of your bodies would not keep you from walking. Standing, you would be more individual. You would oppose the theatre more resolutely. You would give in to fewer illusions. You would suffer more from absentmindedness. You would stand more on the outside. You would be better able to leave yourself to your own devices. You would be less able to imagine represented events as real. The events here would seem less true to life to you. Standing, for example, you would be less able to imagine a death represented on this stage as real. You would be less rigid. You wouldn't let yourself be put under as much of a spell. You wouldn't let as much be put over on you. You wouldn't be satisfied to be mere spectators. It would be easier for you to be of two minds. You could be at two places at once with your thoughts. You could live in two space-time continuums.

We don't want to infect you. We don't want to goad you into a show of feelings. We don't play feelings. We don't embody feelings. We neither laugh nor weep. We don't want to infect you with laughter by laughing or with weeping by laughing or with laughter by weeping or with weeping by weeping. Although laughter is more infectious than weeping, we don't infect you with laughter by laughing. And so forth. We are not playing. We play nothing. We don't modulate. We don't gesticulate. We express ourselves by no means but words. We only speak. We express. We don't express ourselves but the opinion of the author. We express ourselves by speaking. Our speaking is our acting. By speaking, we become theatrical. We are theatrical because we are speaking in a theatre. By always speaking directly to you and by speaking to you of time, of now and of now and of now, we observe the unity of time, place and action. But we observe this unity not only here on stage. Since the stage is no world unto itself, we also observe the unity down where you are. We and you form a unity because we speak directly to you without interruption. Therefore, under certain conditions, we, instead of saying you, could say we. That signifies the unity of action. The stage up here and the auditorium constitute a unity in that they no longer constitute two levels. There is no radiation belt between us. There are no two places here. Here is only one place. That signifies the unity of place. Your time, the time of the spectators and auditors, and our time, the time of the speakers, form a unity in that no other time passes here than your time. Time is not bisected here into played time and play time. Time is not played here. Only real time exists here. Only the time that we, we and you, experience ourselves in our own bodies exists here. Only one time exists here. That signifies the unity of time. All three cited circumstances, taken together, signify the unity of time, place and action. Therefore this piece is classical.

Because we speak to you, you can become conscious of yourself. Because we speak to you, your self-awareness increases. You become aware that you are sitting. You become aware that you are sitting in the theatre. You become aware of the size of your limbs. You become aware of how your limbs are situated. You become aware of your fingers. You become aware of your tongue. You become aware of your throat. You become aware how heavy your head is. You become aware of your sex organs. You become aware of batting your eyelids. You become aware of the muscles with which you swallow. You become aware of the flow of your saliva. You become aware of the beating of your heart. You become aware of raising your eyebrows. You become aware of a prickling sensation on your scalp. You become aware of the impulse to scratch yourself. You become aware of sweating under your armpits. You become aware of your sweaty hands. You become aware of your parched hands. You become aware of the air you are inhaling and exhaling through your mouth and nose. You become aware of our words entering your ears. You acquire presence of mind.

Try not to blink your eyelids. Try not to swallow any more. Try not to move your tongue. Try not to hear anything. Try not to smell anything. Try not to salivate. Try not to sweat. Try not to shift in your seat. Try not to breathe.

Why, you are breathing. Why, you are salivating. Why, you are listening. Why, you are smelling. Why, you are swallowing. Why, you are blinking your eyelids. Why, you are belching. Why, you are sweating. Why, how terribly self-conscious you are.

Don't blink. Don't salivate. Don't bat your eyelashes. Don't inhale. Don't exhale. Don't shift in your seat. Don't listen to us. Don't smell. Don't swallow. Hold your breath.

Swallow. Salivate. Blink. Listen. Breathe.

You are now aware of your presence. You know that it is *your* time that you are spending here. *You* are the topic. You tie the knot. You untie the knot. You are the centre. You are the occasion. You are the reasons why. You provide the initial impulse. You provide us with words here. You are the playmakers and the counterplotters. You are the young comedians. You are the enchanted lovers, you are the ingénues, you are the sentimentalists. You are the grandes dames, you are the character actors, you are the bon vivants and the heroes. You are the heroes and the villains of this piece.

Before you came here, you made certain preparations. You came here with certain preconceptions. You went to the theatre. You prepared yourself to go to the theatre. You had certain expectations. Your thoughts were one step ahead of time. You imagined something. You prepared yourself for something. You prepared yourself to partake in something. You prepared yourself to be seated, to sit on the rented seat and to attend something. Perhaps you had heard of this piece. So you made preparations, you prepared yourself for something. You let events come toward you. You were prepared to sit and have something shown to you.

The rhythm you breathed in was different from ours. You went about dressing yourself in a different manner. You got started in a different way. You approached this location from different directions. You used the public transport system. You came on foot. You came by cab. You used your own means of transport. Before you got under way, you looked at your watch. You expected a telephone call, you picked up the receiver, you turned on the lights, you turned out the lights, you closed doors, you turned keys, you stepped out into the open. You propelled your legs. You let your arms swing up and down as you walked. You walked. You walked from different directions all in the same direction. You found your way here with the help of your sense of direction.

Because of your intention you distinguished yourselves from others who were on their way to other locations. Simply because of your intention, you instantly formed a unit with the others who were on their way to this location. You had the same objective.

You planned to spend a part of your future together with others at a definite time.

You crossed traffic lanes. You looked left and right. You observed traffic signals. You nodded to others. You stopped. You informed others of your destination. You told of your expectations. You communicated your speculations about this piece. You expressed your opinion of this piece. You shook hands. You had others wish you a pleasant evening. You took off your shoes. You held doors open. You had doors held open for you. You met other theatre-goers. You felt like conspirators. You observed the rules of good behaviour. You helped out of coats. You let yourselves be helped out of coats. You stood around. You walked around. You heard the bells. You grew restless. You looked in the mirror. You checked your make-up. You threw sidelong glances. You noticed sidelong glances. You walked. You paced. Your movements became more formal. You heard the bell. You looked at your watch. You became conspirators. You took your seat. You took a look around. You made yourself comfortable. You heard the bell. You stopped chatting. You aligned your glances. You raised your heads. You took a deep breath. You saw the lights dim. You became silent. You heard the doors closing. You stared at the curtain. You waited. You became rigid. You did not move any more. Instead, the curtain moved. You heard the curtain rustling. You were offered an unobstructed view of the stage. Everything was as it always is. Your expectations were not disappointed. You were ready. You leaned back in your seat. The play could begin.

At other times you were also ready. You were on to the game that was being played. You leaned back in your seats. You perceived. You followed. You pursued. You let happen. You let something happen up here that had happened long ago. You watched the past which by means of dialogue and monologue made believe it was contemporaneous. You let yourselves be captivated. You let your-selves become spellbound. You forgot where you were. You forgot the time. You became rigid and remained rigid. You did not move. You did not act. You did not even come up front to see better. You followed no natural impulses. You watched as you watch a beam of light that was produced long before you began to watch. You looked into dead space. You looked at dead points. You experienced a dead time. You heard a dead language. You yourselves were in a dead room in a dead time. It was dead calm. No breath of air moved. You did not move. You stared. The distance between you and us was infinite. We were infinitely far away from you. We moved at an infinite distance from you. We had lived infinitely long before you. We lived up here on the stage before the beginning of time. Your glances and our glances met in infinity. An infinite space was between us. We played. But we did not play with you. You were always posterity here.

Plays were played here. Sense was played here. Nonsense with meaning was played here. The plays here had a background and an underground. They had a false bottom. They were not what they were. They were not what they seemed. There was something behind them. The things and the plot seemed to be, but they were not. They seemed to be as they seemed, but they were different. They did not seem to seem as in a pure play, they seemed to be. They seemed to be reality. The plays here did not pass the time, or they did not only pass the time. They had meaning. They were not timeless like the pure plays, an unreal time passed in them. The conspicuous meaninglessness of some plays was precisely what represented their hidden meaning. Even the pranks of pranksters acquired meaning on these boards. Always something lay in wait. Always something lay in ambush between the words, gestures and props and sought to mean something to you. Always something had two or more meanings. Something was always happening. Something happened in the play that you were supposed to think was real. Stories always happened. A played and unreal time happened. What you saw and heard was supposed to be not only what you saw and heard. It was supposed to be what you did not see and did not hear. Everything was meant. Everything expressed. Even what pretended to express nothing expressed something because something that happens in the theatre expresses something. Everything that was played expressed something real. The play was not played for the play's sake but for the sake of reality. You were to discover a played reality behind the play. You were supposed to fathom the play. Not a play, reality was played. Time was played. Since time was played, reality was played. The theatre played tribunal. The theatre played circus ring. The theatre played moral institution. The theatre played dreams. The theatre played tribal rites. The theatre played mirrors for you. The play exceeded the play. It hinted at reality. It became impure. It meant. Instead of time staying out of play, an unreal and uneffective time transpired. With the unreal time an unreal reality was played. It was not there, it was only signified to you, it was performed. Neither reality nor play transpired here. If a pure play had been played here, time could have been left out of play. A pure play has no time. But since a reality was played, the corresponding time was also played. If a pure play had been played here, there would have been only the time of the spectators here. But since reality was part of the play here, there were always two times: your time, the time of the spectators, and the played time, which seemed to be the real time. But time cannot be played. It cannot be repeated in any play. Time is irretrievable. Time is irresistible. Time is unplayable. Time is real. It cannot be played as real. Since time cannot be played, reality cannot be played either. Only a play where time is left out of play is a play. A play in which time plays a role is no play. Only a timeless play is without meaning. Only a timeless play is self-sufficient. Only a timeless play does not need to *play* time. Only for a timeless play is time without meaning. All other plays are impure plays. There are only plays without time, or plays in which time is real time, like the sixty minutes of a football game, which has only one time because the time of the players is the same time as that of the spectators. All other plays are sham plays. All other plays mirror meretricious facts for you. A timeless play mirrors no facts.

We could do a play within a play for you. We could act out happenings for you that are taking place outside this room during these moments while you are swallowing, while you are batting your eyelashes. We could illustrate the statistics. We could represent what is statistically taking place at other places while you are at this place. By representing what is happening, we could make you imagine these happenings. We could bring them closer to you. We would not need to represent anything that is past. We could play a pure play. For example, we could act out the very process of dying that is statistically happening somewhere at this moment. We could become full of pathos. We could declare that death is the pathos of time, of which we speak all the time. Death could be the pathos of this real time which you are wasting here. At the very least, this play within a play would help bring this piece to a dramatic climax.

But we are not putting anything over on you. We don't imitate. We don't represent any other persons and any other events, even if they statistically exist. We can do without a play of features and a play of gestures. There are no persons who are part of the plot and therefore no impersonators. The plot is not freely invented, for there is no plot. Since there is no plot, accidents are impossible. Similarity with still living or scarcely dead or long-dead persons is not accidental but impossible. For we don't represent anything and are no others than we are. We don't even play ourselves. We are speaking. Nothing is invented here. Nothing is imitated. Nothing is fact. Nothing is left to your imagination.

Owing to the fact that we are not playing and not acting playfully, this piece is half as funny and half as tragic. Owing to the fact that we only speak and don't fall outside time, we cannot depict anything for you and demonstrate nothing for you. We illustrate nothing. We conjure up nothing out of the past. We are not in conflict with the past. We are not in conflict with the present. We don't anticipate the future. In the present, the past, and the future, we speak of time.

That is why, for example, we cannot represent the now and now of dying that is statistically happening now. We cannot represent the gasping for breath that is happening now and now, or the tumbling and falling now, or the death throes, or the grinding of teeth now, or the last words, or the last sigh now, that is statistically happening now this very second, or the last exhalation, or the last ejaculation that is happening now, or the breathlessness that is statistically commencing now, and now, and now, and now, and so on, or the motionlessness now, or the statistically ascertainable rigor mortis, or the lying absolutely quiet now. We cannot represent it. We only speak of it. We are speaking of it *now*.

Owing to the fact that we only speak and owing to the fact that we don't speak of anything invented, we cannot be equivocal or ambiguous. Owing to the fact that we play nothing, there cannot exist two or more levels here or a play within a play. Owing to the fact that we don't gesticulate and don't tell you any stories and don't represent anything, we cannot be poetical. Owing to the fact that we only speak to you, we lose the poetry of ambiguity. For example, we cannot use the gestures and expressions of dying that we mentioned to represent the gestures and expressions of a simultaneously transpiring instance of sexual intercourse that is statistically transpiring now. We can't be equivocal. We cannot play on a false bottom. We cannot remove ourselves from the world. We don't need to be poetic. We don't need to hypnotize you. We don't need to hoodwink you. We don't need to cast an evil eye on you. We don't need a second nature. This is no hypnosis. You don't have to imagine anything. You don't have to dream with open eyes. With the illogic of your dreams you are not dependent on the logic of the stage. The impossibilities of your dreams do not have to confine themselves to the possibilities of the stage. The absurdity of your dreams does not have to obey the authentic laws of the theatre. Therefore we represent neither dreams nor reality. We make claims neither for life nor for dying, neither for society nor for the individual, neither for what is natural nor for what is supernatural, neither for lust nor for grief, neither for reality nor for the play. Time elicits no elegies from us.

This piece is a prologue. It is not the prologue to another piece but the prologue to what you did, what you are doing, and what you will do. You are the topic. This piece is the prologue to the topic. It is the prologue to your practices and customs. It is the prologue to your actions. It is the prologue to your inactivity. It is the prologue to your lying down, to your sitting, to your standing, to your walking. It is the prologue to the plays and to the seriousness of your life. It is also the prologue to your future visits to the theatre. It is also the prologue to all other prologues. This piece is world theatre.

Soon you will move. You will make preparations. You will prepare yourself to applaud. You will prepare yourself not to applaud. When you prepare to do the former, you will clap one hand against the other, that is to say, you will clap one palm to the other palm and repeat these claps in rapid succession. Meanwhile, you will be able to watch your hands clapping or not clapping. You will hear the sound of yourself clapping and the sound of clapping next to you and you will see next to you and in front of you the clapping hands bobbing back and forth or you will not hear the expected clapping and not see the hands bobbing back and forth. Instead, you will perhaps hear other sounds and will yourself produce other sounds. You will prepare to get up. You will hear the seats folding up behind you. You will see us taking our bows. You will see the curtain fall. You will be able to designate the noises the curtain makes during this process. You will pocket your programmes. You will exchange glances. You will exchange words. You will get moving. You will make comments and hear comments. You will suppress comments. You will smile meaningfully. You will smile meaninglessly. You will push in an orderly fashion into the foyer. You will show your cloakroom tickets to redeem your hats and coats. You will stand around. You will see yourselves in mirrors. You will help each other into coats. You will hold doors open for each other. You will say your good-byes. You will accompany. You will be accompanied. You will step into the open. You will return into the everyday. You will go in different directions. If you remain together, you will be a theatre party. You will go to a restaurant. You will think of tomorrow. You will gradually find your way back into reality. You will be able to call reality harsh again. You will be sobered up. You will lead your own lives again. You will no longer be a unit. You will go from one place to different places.

But before you leave you will be insulted.

We will insult you because insulting you is also one way of speaking to you. By insulting you, we can be straight with you. We can switch you on. We can eliminate the free play. We can tear down a wall. We can observe you.

While we are insulting you, you won't just hear us, you will listen to us. The distance between us will no longer be infinite. Due to the fact that we're insulting you, your motionlessness and your rigidity will finally become overt. But we won't insult *you*, we will merely use insulting words which you yourselves use. We will contradict ourselves with our insults. We will mean no one in particular. We will only create an acoustic pattern. You won't have to feel offended. You were warned in advance, so you can feel quite unoffended while we're insulting you. Since you are probably thoroughly offended already, we will waste no more time before thoroughly offending you, you chuckleheads.

You let the impossible become possible. You were the heroes of this piece. You were sparing with your gestures. Your parts were well rounded. Your scenes were unforgettable. You did not play, you *were* the part. You were a happening. You were the find of the evening. You lived your roles. You had the lion's share of the success. You saved the piece. You were a sight. You were a sight to have seen, you bum-lickers.

You were always with it. Your honest toiling didn't help the piece a bit. You contributed only the cues. The best you created was the little you left out. Your silences said everything, you small-timers.

You were thoroughbred actors. You began promisingly. You were true to life. You were realistic. You put everything under your spell. You played us off the stage. You reached Shakespearean heights, you jerks, you skinheads, you scum of the melting pot.

Not one wrong note crossed your lips. You had control of every scene. Your playing was exquisite nobility. Your countenances were of rare exquisiteness. You were a smashing cast. You were a dream cast. You were inimitable, your faces unforgettable. Your sense of humour left us gasping. Your tragedy was of antique grandeur. You gave your best, you spoilsports, you gatecrashers, you fuddy-duddies, you bubbleheads, you powder puffs, you sitting ducks.

You were one of a kind. You had one of your better days tonight. You played ensemble. You were imitations of life, you drips, you diddlers, you atheists, you double-dealers, you fence-sitters, you dirty Jews.

You showed us brand-new vistas. You were well advised to do this piece. You outdid yourselves. You played yourselves loose. You turned yourselves inside out, you lonely crowd, you culture vultures, you nervous nellies, you bronco busters, you moneybags, you potheads, you washouts, you wet blankets, you fire eaters, you generation of freaks, you hopped-up sons and daughters of the revolution, you napalm specialists.

You were priceless. You were a hurricane. You drove shudders up our spines. You swept everything before you, you Colonial hangmen, you savages, you rednecks, you hatchet men, you sub-humans, you fiends, you beasts in human shape, you killer pigs.

You were the right ones. You were breathtaking. You did not disappoint our wildest hopes. You were born actors. Play-acting was in your blood, you butchers, you buggers, you bullshitters, you bullies, you rabbits, you fuck-offs, you farts.

You had perfect breath-control, you windbags, you waspish wasps, you wags, you gargoyles, you tackheads, you milksops, you mickey-mice, you chicken-shits, you cheap skates, you wrong numbers, you zeros, you back numbers, you one-shots, you centipedes, you supernumeraries, you superfluous lives, you crumbs, you cardboard figures, you *pain* in the mouth.

You are accomplished actors, you hucksters, you traitors to your country, you embezzlers, you would-be revolutionaries, you re-actionaries, you conshies, you ivory-tower artists, you defeatists, you massive retaliators, you white-rabbit pacifists, you nihilists, you individualists, you Communists, you vigilantes, you socialists, you minute men, you whiz-kids, you turtledoves, you crazy hawks, you stool pigeons, you worms, you antediluvian monstrosities, you claqueurs, you clique of babbits, you rabble, you blubber, you quivering reeds, you wretches, you ofays, you oafs, you spooks, you blackbaiters, you cooky pushers, you abortions, you bitches and bastards, you nothings, you thingamajigs.

O you cancer victims, O you haemorrhoid sufferers, O you multiple

sclerotics, O you syphilitics, O you cardiac conditions, O you para-
plegics, O you catatonics, O you schizoids, O you paranoids, O
you hypochondriacs, O you carriers of causes of death, O you
suicide candidates, O you potential peacetime casualties, O you
potential war dead, O you potential accident victims, O you potential increase in the mortality rate, O you potential dead.

You wax figures. You impersonators. You bad-hats. You troupers.
You tear-jerkers. You potboilers. You foul mouths. You sell-outs.
You deadbeats. You phonies. You milestones in the history of the
theatre. You historic moments. You immortal souls. You positive
heroes. You abortionists. You anti-heroes. You everyday heroes.
You luminaries of science. You beacons in the dark. You educated
gasbags. You cultivated classes. You befuddled aristocrats. You
rotten middle class. You lowbrows. You people of our time. You
children of the world. You sadsacks. You church and lay digni-
taries. You wretches. You congressmen. You commissioners. You
scoundrels. You generals. You lobbyists. You Chiefs of Staff. You
chairmen of this and that. You tax evaders. You presidential
advisers. You U-2 pilots. You agents. You corporate-military
establishment. You entrepreneurs. You Eminencies. You Excel-
lencies. You Holiness. Mr President. You crowned heads. You
pushers. You architects of the future. You builders of a better
world. You mafiosos. You wiseacres. You smart-alecs. You who
embrace life. You who detest life. You who have no feeling about
life. You ladies and gents you, you celebrities of public and
cultural life you, you who are present you, you brothers and sisters
you, you comrades you, you worthy listeners you, you fellow
humans you.

You were welcome here. We thank you. Good night.

*The curtain falls at once. However, it does not remain closed but
rises again immediately regardless of the behaviour of the public. The
speakers stand and look at the public without looking at anyone in*

*particular. Roaring applause and wild whistling is piped in through the loudspeakers; to this, one might add taped audience reactions to pop-music concerts. The deafening howling and yelling lasts until the public begins to leave. Only then does the curtain descend once and for all.*

# Self-Accusation

*for Libgart*

*This piece is a* Sprechstück *for one male and one female speaker. It has no roles. Female and male speaker, whose voices are attuned to each other, alternate or speak together, quiet and loud, with abrupt transitions, thus producing an acoustic order. The stage is empty. The two speakers use microphones and loudspeakers. The auditorium and the stage are lighted throughout. The curtain is not used at any time, not even at the end of the piece.*

I came into the world.

I became. I was begotten. I originated. I grew. I was born. I was entered in the birth register. I grew older.

I moved. I moved parts of my body. I moved my body. I moved on one and the same spot. I moved from the spot. I moved from one spot to another. I had to move. I was able to move.

I moved my mouth. I came to my senses. I made myself notice-able. I screamed. I spoke. I heard noises. I distinguished between noises. I produced noises. I produced sounds. I produced tones. I was able to produce tones, noises and sounds. I was able to speak. I was able to scream. I was able to remain silent.

I saw. I saw what I had seen before. I became conscious. I recog-nized what I had seen before. I recognized what I had recognized before. I perceived. I perceived what I had perceived before. I became conscious. I recognized what I had perceived before.

I looked. I saw objects. I looked at indicated objects. I indicated indicated objects. I learned the designation of indicated objects. I designated indicated objects. I learned the designation of objects that cannot be indicated. I learned. I remembered. I remembered the signs I learned. I saw designated forms. I designated similar forms with the same name. I designated differences between dissimilar forms. I designated absent forms. I learned to fear absent forms. I learned to wish for the presence of absent forms. I learned the words 'to wish' and 'to fear'.

I learned. I learned the words. I learned the verbs. I learned the difference between being and having been. I learned the nouns. I learned the difference between singular and plural. I learned the adverbs. I learned the difference between here and there. I learned the demonstrative pronouns. I learned the difference between this and that. I learned the adjectives. I learned the difference between good and evil. I learned the possessives. I learned the difference between mine and yours. I acquired a vocabulary.

I became the object of sentences. I became the attribute of sentences. I became the object and the attribute of main and subordinate clauses. I became the movement of a mouth. I became a sequence of letters of the alphabet.

I said my name. I said I. I crawled on all fours. I ran. I ran toward something. I ran away from something. I stood up. I stepped out of the passive mode. I became active. I walked at approximately a right angle to the earth. I leapt. I defied the force of gravity. I learned to relieve myself outside my clothes. I learned to bring my body under my control. I learned to control myself.

I learned to be able. I was able. I was able to want. I was able to walk on two legs. I was able to walk on my hands. I was able to remain. I was able to remain upright. I was able to remain prone. I was able to crawl on my stomach. I was able to play dead. I was able to hold my breath. I was able to kill myself. I was able to spit. I was able to nod. I was able to say no. I was able to perform gestures. I was able to question. I was able to answer questions. I was able to imitate. I was able to follow an example. I was able to play. I was able to do something. I was able to fail to do something. I was able to destroy objects. I was able to picture objects to myself. I was able to value objects. I was able to speak objects. I was able to speak about objects. I was able to remember objects.

I lived in time. I thought of beginning and end. I thought of myself. I thought of others. I stepped out of nature. I became. I became unnatural. I came to my history. I recognized that I am not you. I was able to tell my history. I was able to conceal my history.

I was able to want something. I was able not to want something.

I made myself. I made myself what I am. I changed myself. I became someone else. I became responsible for my history. I became co-responsible for the histories of the others. I became one history among others. I made the world into my own. I became sensible.

I no longer had to obey only nature. I was supposed to comply with rules. I was supposed to. I was supposed to comply with mankind's historic rules. I was supposed to act. I was supposed to fail to act. I was supposed to let happen. I learned rules. I learned as a metaphor for rules 'the snares of rules'. I learned rules for behaviour and for thoughts. I learned rules for inside and outside. I learned rules for things and people. I learned general and specific rules. I learned rules for this world and the afterworld. I learned rules for air, water, fire and earth. I learned the rules and the exceptions to the rules. I learned the basic rules and the derivative rules. I learned to pretend. I became fit for society.

I became: I was supposed to. I became capable of eating with my hands: I was supposed to avoid soiling myself. I became capable of adopting other people's practices: I was supposed to avoid my own malpractices. I became capable of distinguishing between hot and cold: I was supposed to avoid playing with fire. I became capable of separating good and evil: I was supposed to eschew evil. I became capable of playing according to the rules: I was supposed to avoid an infraction of the rules of the game. I became capable of realizing the unlawfulness of my actions and of acting in accordance with this realization: I was supposed to eschew criminal acts. I became capable of using my sexual powers: I was supposed to avoid misusing my sexual powers.

*       *       *

I was included in all the rules. With my personal data I became part of the record. With my soul I became tainted by original sin. With my lottery number I was inscribed in the lottery lists. With my illnesses I was filed in the hospital ledger. With my firm I was entered in the commercial register. With my distinguishing marks I was retained in the personnel records.

I came of age. I became fit to act. I became fit to sign a contract. I became fit to have a last will and testament.

As of a moment in time I could commit sins. As of another moment I became liable to prosecution. As of another moment I could lose my honour. As of another moment I could oblige myself contractually to do or to abstain from doing something.

I became duty-bound to atone. I became duty-bound to have an address. I became duty-bound to make restitution. I became duty-bound to pay taxes. I became duty-bound to do military service. I became duty-bound to do my duty. I became duty-bound to go to school. I became duty-bound to be vaccinated. I became duty-bound to care. I became duty-bound to pay my bills. I became duty-bound to be investigated. I became duty-bound to be educated. I became duty-bound to give proof. I became duty-bound to be insured. I became duty-bound to have an identity. I became duty-bound to be registered. I became duty-bound to pay maintenance. I became duty-bound to execute. I became duty-bound to testify.

I became. I became responsible. I became guilty. I became pardonable. I had to atone for my history. I had to atone for my past. I had to atone for the past. I had to atone for my time. I came into the world only with time.

Which demands of time did I violate? Which demands of practical reason did I violate? Which secret paragraphs did I violate?

Which programmes did I violate? Which eternal laws of the universe did I violate? Which laws of the underworld did I violate? Which of the most primitive rules of common decency did I violate? Which and whose party lines did I violate? Which laws of the theatre did I violate? Which vital interests did I violate? Which unspoken law did I violate? Which unwritten law did I violate? Which command of the hour did I violate? Which rules of life did I violate? Which common-sense rules did I violate? Which rules of love did I violate? Which rules of the game did I violate? Which rules of cosmetics did I violate? Which laws of aesthetics did I violate? Which laws of the stronger did I violate? Which commands of piety did I violate? Which law of the outlaws did I violate? Which desire for change did I violate? Which law of the world and the afterworld did I violate? Which rule of orthography did I violate? Which right of the past did I violate? Which law of free fall did I violate? Did I violate the rules, plans, ideas, postulates, basic principles, etiquettes, general propositions, opinions and formulas of the whole world?

I did. I failed to do. I let do. I expressed myself. I expressed myself through ideas. I expressed myself through expressions. I expressed myself before myself. I expressed myself before myself and others. I expressed myself before the impersonal power of the law and of good conduct. I expressed myself before the personal power of God.

I expressed myself in movements. I expressed myself in actions. I expressed myself in motionlessness. I expressed myself in inaction.

I signified. I signified with each of my expressions. With each of my expressions I signified the fulfilment or disregard of rules.

I expressed myself by spitting. I expressed myself by showing disapproval. I expressed myself by showing approval. I expressed myself by relieving nature. I expressed myself by discarding useless and used objects. I expressed myself by killing live beings. I expressed myself by destroying objects. I expressed myself by breathing. I expressed myself by sweating. I expressed myself by secreting snot and tears.

I spat. I spat out. I spat with an aim. I spat at. I spat on the floor in places where it was improper to spit on the floor. I spat on the floor in places where spitting was a violation of health regulations. I spat in the face of people whom it was a personal insult of God to spit at. I spat on objects which it was a personal insult of human beings to spit upon. I did not spit in front of people when spitting out before them allegedly brought good luck. I did not spit in front of cripples. I did not spit at actors before their performance. I did not use the spittoon. I expectorated in waiting rooms. I spat against the wind.

I expressed approval in places where the expression of approval was prohibited. I expressed disapproval at times when the expression of disapproval was not desired. I expressed disapproval and approval in places and at times when the expression of disapproval and the expression of approval were intolerable. I failed to express approval at times when the expression of approval was called for. I expressed approval during a difficult trapeze act in the circus. I expressed approval inopportunely.

I discarded used and useless objects in places where discarding objects was prohibited. I deposited objects in places where depositing objects was punishable. I stored objects in places where storing objects was reprehensible. I failed to deliver objects I was legally obligated to deliver. I threw objects out the window of a moving train. I failed to throw litter into litter baskets. I left litter lying in the woods. I threw burning cigarettes into hay. I failed to hand over pamphlets dropped by enemy planes.

*     *     *

I expressed myself by speaking. I expressed myself by appropriating objects. I expressed myself by reproducing live beings. I expressed myself by producing objects. I expressed myself by looking. I expressed myself by playing. I expressed myself by walking.

I walked. I walked purposelessly. I walked purposefully. I walked on paths. I walked on paths on which it was prohibited to walk. I failed to walk on paths when it was imperative to do so. I walked on paths on which it was sinful to walk purposelessly. I walked purposefully when it was imperative to walk purposelessly. I walked on paths on which it was prohibited to walk with an objective. I walked. I walked even when walking was prohibited and against custom. I walked through passages through which it was an act of conformity to pass. I stepped on property on which it was a disgrace to step. I stepped on to property without my identity papers when it was prohibited to step on it without identity papers. I left buildings which it was a lack of solidarity to leave. I entered buildings which it was unseemly to enter without a covered head. I stepped on territory which it was prohibited to step upon. I visited the territory of a state which it was prohibited to visit. I left the territory of a state which it was a hostile act to leave. I drove into streets in a direction it was undisciplined to enter. I walked in directions it was illegal to walk in. I went so far that it was inadvisable to go farther. I stopped when it was impolite to stop. I walked on the right of persons when it was thoughtless to walk on their right. I sat down on seats that were reserved for others to sit on. I failed to walk on when ordered to walk on. I walked slowly when it was imperative to walk quickly. I failed to get on my feet when it was imperative to get on my feet. I lay down in places where it was forbidden to lie down. I stopped at demonstrations. I walked on by when it was imperative to offer help. I entered no-man's-land. I lay down on the floor when there was an R in the month. I delayed people's flight by walking slowly in narrow hallways. I jumped off moving buses. I opened the carriage door before the train had come to a complete stop.

I spoke. I spoke out. I spoke out what others thought. I only thought what others spoke out. I gave expression to public opinion. I falsified public opinion. I spoke at places where it was impious to speak. I spoke loudly at places where it was inconsiderate to speak loudly. I whispered when it was required to speak up. I remained silent at times when silence was a disgrace. I spoke as a public speaker when it was imperative to speak as a private person. I spoke with persons with whom it was dishonourable to speak. I greeted people whom it was a betrayal of principle to greet. I spoke in a language which it was a hostile act to use. I spoke about objects of which it was tactless to speak. I suppressed my knowledge of a crime. I failed to speak well of the dead. I spoke ill of absent persons. I spoke without being asked to. I spoke to soldiers on duty. I spoke to the driver during the trip.

I failed to observe the rules of the language. I committed linguistic blunders. I used words thoughtlessly. I blindly attributed qualities to the objects in the world. I blindly attributed to the words for the objects words for the qualities of the objects. I regarded the world blindly with the words for the qualities of the objects. I called objects dead. I called complexity lively. I called melancholy black. I called madness bright. I called passion hot. I called anger red. I called the ultimate questions unanswerable. I called the milieu genuine. I called nature free. I called horror frightful. I called laughter liberating. I called freedom inalienable. I called loyalty proverbial. I called fog milky, I called the surface smooth. I called severity Old Testament-like. I called the sinner poor. I called dignity inborn. I called the bomb menacing. I called the doctrine salutary. I called darkness impenetrable. I called morality hypocritical. I called lines of demarcation vague. I called the raised forefinger moralistic. I called mistrust creative. I called trust blind. I called the atmosphere sober. I called conflict productive. I called conclusions futuristic. I called integrity intellectual. I called capitalism corrupt. I called emotions murky. I called the picture of the world distorted. I called ideology false. I called the view of the world fuzzy. I called criticism constructive. I called science unbiased. I called precision scientific. I called eyes sparkling. I called results easily obtainable. I called the dialogue useful. I called dogma rigid. I called the discussion necessary. I called opinion subjective. I called pathos hollow. I called mysticism obscure. I called thoughts unripe. I called horseplay foolish. I called monotony oppressive. I called results obvious. I called being true. I called truth profound. I called lies shallow. I called life rich. I called money of no account. I called reality vulgar. I called the moment delicious. I called war just. I called peace lazy. I called weight dead. I called conflicts irreconcilable. I called the fronts fixed. I called the universe curved. I called snow white. I called ice cold. I called spheres round. I called a something certain. I called the measure full.

I appropriated objects. I acquired objects as property and possessions. I appropriated objects at places where the appropriation of objects was prohibited on principle. I appropriated objects which it was an act hostile to society to appropriate. I claimed objects as private property when it was inopportune to claim I owned them. I declared objects to be public property when it was unethical to remove them from private hands. I treated objects without care when it was prescribed to treat them with care. I touched objects which it was unaesthetic and sinful to touch. I separated objects from objects which it was inadvisable to separate. I failed to keep the required distance from objects from which it was imperative to keep the required distance. I treated persons like objects. I treated animals like persons. I took up contact with living beings with whom it was immoral to take up contact. I touched objects with objects which it was useless to bring into touch with each other. I traded with living beings and objects with which it was inhuman to trade. I treated fragile goods without care. I connected the positive pole to the positive pole. I used externally applicable medicine internally. I touched exhibited objects. I tore scabs off half-healed wounds. I touched electric wires. I failed to register letters that had to be sent registered. I failed to affix a stamp to applications that required a stamp. I failed to wear mourning clothes upon a death in the family. I failed to use skin cream to protect my skin from the sun. I dealt in slaves. I dealt in uninspected meat. I climbed mountains with shoes unfit for mountain climbing. I failed to wash fresh fruit. I failed to disinfect the clothes of plague victims. I failed to shake the hair lotion before use.

I looked and listened. I looked at. I looked at objects which it was shameless to look at. I failed to look at objects which it was a dereliction of duty to fail to look at. I failed to watch events which it was philistine to fail to watch. I failed to watch events in the position prescribed to watch them I failed to avert my eyes during events it was treasonable to watch. I looked back when looking back was proof of a bad upbringing. I looked away when it was cowardly to look away. I listened to persons whom it was unprincipled to listen to. I inspected forbidden areas. I inspected buildings in danger of collapse. I failed to look at persons who were speaking to me. I failed to look at persons with whom I was speaking. I watched unadvisable and objectionable movies. I heard information in the mass media that was hostile to the state. I watched games without a ticket. I stared at strangers. I looked without dark glasses into the sun. I kept my eyes open during sexual intercourse.

I ate. I ate more than I could stomach. I drank more than my bladder could hold. I consumed food and drink. I ingested the four elements. I inhaled and exhaled the four elements. I ate at moments when it was undisciplined to eat. I failed to breathe in the prescribed manner. I breathed air which it was below my station to breathe. I inhaled when it was harmful to inhale. I ate meat during the fast days. I breathed without a gas mask. I ate on the street. I inhaled exhaust gases. I ate without knife and fork. I failed to leave myself time to breathe. I ate the Host with my teeth. I failed to breathe through my nose.

I played. I played wrong. I played according to rules which, according to existing rules, were against convention. I played at times and places where it was asocial and ingenuous to play. I played with persons with whom it was dishonourable to play. I played with objects with which it was unceremonious to play. I failed to play at times and places where it was unsociable to fail to play. I played according to the rules when it was individualistic not to play according to the rules. I played with myself when it would have been humane to play with others. I played with powers with whom it was presumptuous to play. I failed to play seriously. I played too seriously. I played with fire. I played with lighters. I played with marked cards. I played with human lives. I played with spray cans. I played with life. I played with feelings. I played myself. I played without chips. I failed to play during playtime. I played with the inclination to evil. I played with my thoughts. I played with the thought of suicide. I played on a thin sheet of ice. I played and trespassed at one and the same time. I played despair. I played with my despair. I played with my sex organ. I played with words. I played with my fingers.

I came into the world afflicted with original sin. My very nature inclined toward evil. My innate viciousness expressed itself at once in envy of my fellow suckling. One day in the world, I was no longer free of sin. Bawling, I craved my mother's breasts. All I knew was to suck. All I knew was to gratify my desires. With my reason I refused to recognize the laws that were placed in the universe and in myself. I was conceived in malice. I was begotten in malice. I expressed my malice by destroying things. I expressed my malice by trampling live beings to death. I was disobedient out of love of play. What I loved in playing was the sense of

winning. I loved in fantastic stories the itch in my ear. I idolized
people. I took greater delight in the trivia of poets than in useful
knowledge. I feared a solecism more than the eternal laws. I let
myself be governed solely by my palate. I only trusted my senses.
I failed to prove that I had a sense of reality. I not only loved
crimes, I loved committing crimes. I preferred to do evil in company. I loved accomplices. I loved complicity. I loved sin for its
danger. I did not search for truth. The pleasure I took in art was
in my pain and my compassion. I pandered to the desires of my
eyes. I failed to recognize the purpose of history. I was godfor-
saken. I was forsaken by the world. I did not designate the world
as *this* world. I also included the heavenly bodies in the world. I
was sufficient for myself. I cared only for worldly things. I took no
cold bath against melancholy. I took no hot bath against passion. I
used my body for wrong ends. I failed to take notice of the facts.
I failed to subordinate my physical nature to my spiritual nature.
I denied my nature. I ran up against the nature of things. I indiscriminately sought power. I indiscriminately sought money. I
failed to teach myself to regard money as a means. I lived in excess
of my means. I failed to have the means to put up with the state of
affairs. I myself determined how I would fashion my life. I did not
overcome myself. I did not toe the line. I disturbed the eternal
order. I failed to recognize that evil is only the absence of good. I
failed to recognize that evil is only an abuse. I gave birth to death
in my sins. I made myself, with my sins, one with the cattle that is
to be slaughtered in the slaughterhouse but snuffles at the very
iron designed to slaughter it. I failed to resist the beginnings. I
failed to find the moment to stop. I made myself an image of the
highest being. I sought not to make myself an image of the highest
being. I refused to divulge the name of the highest being. I only
believed in the three persons of grammar. I told myself that there
is no higher being so as not to have to fear it. I looked for the
opportunity. I did not use the chance. I did not submit to necessity. I did not count on the possibility. I did not learn from bad
examples. I did not learn from the past. I abandoned myself to the

free play of forces. I mistook freedom for license. I mistook honesty for self-exposure. I mistook obscenity for originality. I mistook the dream for reality. I mistook life for the cliché. I mistook coercion for necessary guidance. I mistook love for instinct. I mistook the cause for the effect. I failed to observe the unity of thought and action. I failed to see things as they really are. I succumbed to the magic of the moment. I failed to regard existence as a provisional gift. I broke my word. I did not have command of the language. I did not reject the world. I did not affirm authority. I was a naïve believer in authority. I did not husband my sexual powers. I sought lust as an end in itself. I was not sure of myself. I became a puzzle to myself. I wasted my time. I overslept my time. I wanted to stop time. I wanted to speed up time. I was in conflict with time. I did not want to grow older. I did not want to die. I did not let things come toward me. I could not limit myself. I was impatient. I could not wait for it. I did not think of the future. I did not think of *my* future. I lived from one moment to the next. I was domineering. I behaved as though I was alone in the world. I proved ill-bred. I was self-willed. I lacked a will of my own. I did not work on myself. I failed to make work the basis of my existence. I failed to see God in every beggar. I did not eradicate evil at its roots. I irresponsibly thrust children into the world. I failed to adapt my pleasures to my social circumstances. I sought for bad company. I always wanted to be at the centre. I was too much alone. I was not enough alone. I led my own life too much. I failed to grasp the meaning of the word 'too'. I failed to regard the happiness of all mankind as my ultimate aim. I did not place the common interest before the individual interest. I did not face the music. I disregarded orders. I failed to disobey unjustifiable orders. I did not know my limits. I failed to see things in their relationship with one another. I made no virtue of necessity. I switched convictions. I was incorrigible. I failed to put myself at the service of the cause. I was satisfied with the status quo. I saw no one but myself. I yielded to insinuations. I decided neither for one nor for the other. I took no stand. I disturbed the balance of power. I violated generally acknowledged principles. I did not fulfil the quota. I fell behind the goal that had been set. I was one and everything to myself. I did not take enough fresh air. I woke up too late. I did not clean the pavement. I left doors unlocked. I stepped too near the cage. I failed to keep entrances free. I failed to keep exits free. I pulled the communication cord without a proper reason. I leaned bicycles against forbidden walls. I solicited and peddled. I did not keep the streets clean. I did not take off my shoes. I leaned out the window of a moving train. I handled open fires in rooms that were fire-traps. I paid unannounced visits. I did not get up for invalids. I lay down in a hotel bed with a lighted cigarette. I failed to turn off taps. I spent nights on park benches. I failed to keep dogs on a lead. I failed to muzzle dogs that bit. I failed to leave umbrellas and coats in the cloakroom. I touched goods before I bought them. I failed to close containers immediately after use. I tossed pressurized containers into the fire. I crossed on the red. I walked on motorways. I walked along the railway track. I failed to walk on the pavement. I failed to pass right down inside buses. I did not hold on to the straps. I used the toilet while the train was standing in the station. I did not follow the instructions of the staff. I started motor vehicles where it was prohibited to do so. I failed to push buttons. I crossed the rails in railway stations. I failed to step back when trains were coming in. I exceeded the load limit in lifts. I disturbed the quiet of the night. I affixed posters to forbidden walls. I tried to open doors by pushing when they could only be pulled open. I tried to open doors by pulling when they could only be pushed open. I roamed the streets after dark. I lit lights during blackouts. I did not remain calm in accidents. I left the house during curfew. I did not remain at my post during catastrophes. I thought of myself first. I indiscriminately rushed out of rooms. I activated alarm signals without authorization. I destroyed alarm signals without authorization. I failed to use emergency exits. I pushed. I trampled. I failed to break the window with the hammer. I blocked the way. I put up unauthorized resistance. I did not stop when challenged. I did not raise my hands above my head. I did not aim at the legs. I played with the trigger of a cocked gun. I failed to save women and children first. I approached the drowning from behind. I kept my hands in my pockets. I took no evasive action. I did not let myself be blindfolded. I did not look for cover. I offered an easy target. I was too slow. I was too fast. I *moved.*

I did not regard the movement of my shadow as proof of the movement of the earth. I did not regard my fear of the dark as proof of my existence. I did not regard the demands of reason for immortality as proof of life after death. I did not regard my nausea at the thought of the future as proof of my non-existence after death. I did not regard subsiding pain as proof of the passage of time. I did not regard my lust for life as proof that time stands still.

I am not what I was. I was not what I should have been. I did not become what I should have become. I did not keep what I should have kept.

I went to the theatre. I heard this piece. I spoke this piece. I wrote this piece.

## Methuen Playscripts

\*    \*    \*

## Methuen's Theatre Classics